A BEACON BIOGRAPHY

Cam Newton

Pete DiPrimio

Copyright © 2017 by Purple Toad Publishing, Inc. All rights reserved. No part of this book may be reproduced without written permission from the publisher. Printed and bound in the United States of America.

Printing   1   2   3   4   5   6   7   8   9

A Beacon Biography

Angelina Jolie
Big Time Rush
Cam Newton
Carly Rae Jepsen
Daisy Ridley
Drake
Ed Sheeran
Ellen DeGeneres
Elon Musk
Harry Styles of One Direction
Jennifer Lawrence
John Boyega
Kevin Durant
Lorde
Malala
Maria von Trapp
Markus "Notch" Persson, Creator of Minecraft
Mo'ne Davis
Muhammad Ali
Neil deGrasse Tyson
Peyton Manning
Robert Griffin III (RG3)

Publisher's Cataloging-in-Publication Data
DiPrimio, Pete.
   Cam Newton / written by Pete DiPrimio.
      p. cm.
Includes bibliographic references, glossary, and index.
ISBN 9781624692628
1. Newton, Cam, 1989– —Juvenile literature. 2. Football players—United States—Biography—Juvenile literature. 3. Quarterbacks (Football)--United States --Juvenile literature. I. Series: Beacon biography.
  GV939.N42 2017
  796.332092

Library of Congress Control Number: 2016937027

eBook ISBN: 9781624692635

ABOUT THE AUTHOR: Pete DiPrimio is an award-winning sports writer for the *Fort Wayne (Indiana) News-Sentinel*, a long-time freelance writer, and a member of the Indiana Sportswriters and Sports broadcasters Hall of Fame. He has been an adjunct lecturer for the National Sports Journalism Center at IUPU-Indianapolis and for Indiana University's School of Journalism. He is the author of three nonfiction books pertaining to Indiana University athletics and more than 20 children's books. Pete is also a fitness instructor, plus a tennis, racquetball, biking, and weightlifting enthusiast.

PUBLISHER'S NOTE: This story has not been authorized or endorsed by Cam Newton.

CONTENTS

Chapter One
Superman Finds His Kryptonite 5

Chapter Two
Making a Bigger Shadow 9

Chapter Three
An NFL Star Is Born 15

Chapter Four
Super Bowl Lesson 19

Chapter Five
Beyond the Field 23

Statistics 26

Chronology 27

Chapter Notes 28

Further Reading 29

Books 29

On the Internet 29

Works Consulted 29

Glossary 31

Index 32

Carolina quarterback Cam Newton has never been a good loser. He was especially angry during his interview after losing the Super Bowl in February of 2016 to Denver. He finally walked out, and later apologized.

Chapter 1

Superman Finds His Kryptonite

Cam Newton slouched in a chair, surrounded by microphones and cameras, the hood of a Carolina Panthers grayish blue sweatshirt shadowing his face. Questions came and his answers were clipped and short. He sighed and pressed his lips. He stared without seeming to see.

Welcome to the aftermath of Carolina's 24-10 Super Bowl loss to Denver.

As the NFL's most valuable player, the dual-threat Superman of a quarterback had dominated the 2015 season in record fashion. Cam was a symbol of the league, a leader by deed who needed to show it by word.

On February 7, 2016, in Santa Clara, California, he wasn't ready. The Denver Broncos sacked him six times and hit him on nearly every play, with millions of people around the world watching. Poor play, and the disappointment of losing a game the Panthers were favored to win, left Newton angry and upset.

Even worse, Denver cornerback Chris Harris was being interviewed right behind him. Cam could hear Harris talking about how the Broncos had shut down the Panthers.

A reporter asked Cam what his message was to Panthers fans.

"We'll be back."

Q: Can you explain why Carolina didn't play its normal game?

"Got outplayed."

Q: Why?

"Got outplayed, bro."

Q: Did Denver do anything different?

"Nothing different."

Q: Do we sometimes forget that defenses can dominate offenses?

"No."

Q: Did you see anything that you didn't expect?

"They just played better than us. I don't know what you want me to say. They made more plays than us, and that's what it comes down to. We had our opportunities. It wasn't nothing special that they did. We dropped balls; we turned the ball over; gave up sacks; threw errant passes. That's it. They scored more points than us."

Q: Can you describe your disappointment?

"We lost."

Q: This has to be real tough.

Cam couldn't take it anymore. "I'm done, man," he said, and walked out.[1]

Criticism followed.

"You can't do that," TV announcer Deion Sanders said to a national audience. "You're the face of this league. You can't do that."[2]

As an NFL Hall of Fame defensive back, Sanders' words had impact.

Later, ESPN commentator Jalen Rose, a former NBA player, told *Ebony* magazine, "As soon as he took the stage, we all knew he was pouting because he had the hoodie on. If he got up there and handled it like a boss, no one would have said anything."[3]

Two days after the Super Bowl, Cam explained his behavior. He said he was a "sore

Deion Sanders

loser" and that if he had offended anyone, "that's cool."⁴

He also said he's human and that his job is to win games and not a "popularity contest."⁵

Carolina coach Ron Rivera said the criticism of Cam was unfair, that people needed to look at all the good the quarterback had done, which included going out of his way to help sick and hurting kids.

Cam was 27 years old in February of 2016, a veteran of major college football and of five NFL seasons. He was the 2010 Heisman Trophy winner and the number one NFL draft pick in 2011. He was so good that he jokingly wore Superman shirts—which didn't mean he didn't make mistakes. The press conference showed a weakness. He knew he had to learn how to be a leader, how to make his teammates better, how to handle the bad with the good.

Ron Rivera

"He is maturing as a man," Rivera told ESPN. "People draw something on a snapshot. Don't take a snapshot. Take the whole album."⁶

Cam is a superstar, but not a saint. He is a great athlete, an imperfect man, and a hero who angers as well as inspires.

"I am an African American quarterback," he said in the days before the Super Bowl. "That might scare some people because they haven't seen anything they can compare it to."⁷ He apparently forgot about the other successful African American quarterbacks.

Cam dances after touchdowns. The dance is called the dab. He sticks his arms to the side, thrusts his nose in his elbow, and flashes a 50,000-watt smile. If not everybody likes it, well, Cam can live with that.

Cam is rich in success, toughened by mistakes. He is also more than that. He is a person who makes a difference in other people's lives.

Cam enjoys a moment with his father, Cecil Sr., in downtown College Park near Atlanta. Cam also has a close relationship with older brother, Cecil Jr. (below). His father and brother also were outstanding football players.

Chapter 2

Making a Bigger Shadow

Cameron Jerrell Newton was born on May 11, 1989, in College Park, a city near Atlanta, Georgia. His father, Cecil Sr., was a football player at Savannah State. In the mid-1980s, he was good enough to try out for the NFL's Dallas Cowboys and the Buffalo Bills. Cam's older brother, Cecil Jr., played center in the NFL. By 2016, their younger brother, Caylin, had become a talented high school quarterback in Atlanta.

Cam started playing organized football when he was seven. By then he was nearly 5 feet tall and weighed almost 100 pounds, nearly too big for the league and good enough to out-play older kids. People often asked to see his birth certificate because they thought he was too old for the team. He often played on offense and defense (as a hard-hitting linebacker), although quarterback was his best position.

He was smart and popular at Seaborn Lee Elementary School and Camp Creek Middle School, but he had so much energy, he sometimes struggled to pay attention in class and to focus on his grades. His parents, especially his mother, Jackie, made sure he kept working at it.

By the time Cam got to Seaborn Lee Elementary School near Atlanta, he was already drawing attention because of his multi-sport talents.

Cam was also a good baseball and basketball player. He gave up baseball (he was a talented centerfielder) because he was afraid of getting hit by pitches.

Cam was by far the best player on his youth football team, in part because he was so much bigger than the other players.

"My mom always wondered how I could be afraid of a little baseball when I always had these huge guys chasing me (in football)," he told ESPN. "It's a good question."[1]

By the time Cam got to Westlake High School near Atlanta, football had become his number one sport. Coach Dallas Allen was impressed enough to put him on the varsity team as a freshman. Others, though, kept comparing him to his brother Cecil, who was three years older and had earned a scholarship to Tennessee State. Cam got tired of that. It helped make him tougher and more determined.

Meanwhile, he got bigger and stronger, so much so that he became a five-star prospect, the top national level. As a 6-foot-4, 230-pound senior, he was considered the nation's number two dual-threat quarterback, which meant he was good at passing and running. Newton could throw the ball 75 yards, and he was so big and fast, no one could tackle him.

He knew he was good, but he didn't want to make a big deal about it. Unlike other players, he did not make highlight videos of his games.

"My talent spoke for itself," he told ESPN. "My mentality was like, 'If you come see me, then I'll put on a show for you.' That wasn't cockiness or arrogance. That's just me speaking with confidence, saying that if you come see me, I'll hold myself accountable enough to play at a high level."[2]

Cam was so good in high school that some of the top college programs in the country recruited him, including Florida, Oklahoma, Georgia, Mississippi and Mississippi State. He finally picked Florida.

Some college coaches recruited Cam as a running quarterback. Others wanted him as more of a passer. At Auburn University in Alabama, Coach Tommy Tuberville wanted him as a tight end so that he could block and catch passes.

Cam didn't want to do that. He liked the Florida Gators, who had a big quarterback in Tim Tebow. As a freshman in 2007, Cam was Tebow's backup. In 2008, Cam hurt his ankle and didn't play, while Tebow led the Gators to the national championship.

In November of that year, Cam was accused of stealing a laptop. He denied it, saying he had bought it from someone for $120, and should have known the deal was too good to be true.

However, when police came to his room, he threw the laptop out the window. Police charged him with burglary, larceny, and obstruction of justice. The charges were eventually dropped, but Florida coach Urban Meyer suspended him. Reports surfaced that Cam was on the verge of being kicked out of school for three instances of cheating in class.

Cam transferred to Blinn College in Texas. In his one season there he passed for 2,833 yards, ran for 655 more, and totaled 38 touchdowns. He led Blinn to the 2009 junior college national championship and earned junior college All-America honors.

Auburn again wanted him, but this time with a new coach. Gene Chizik saw him as a big-time quarterback similar to two others he had coached, Vince Young and Daunte Culpepper. These two college stars had gone on to play in the NFL.

Cam chose Auburn, and controversy followed. A former Mississippi State quarterback said a man connected to an NFL agent was trying to get a college to pay Cam to join its program. This type of payment is against NCAA rules. ESPN reported that one offer was for $180,000. The Newton family denied it. There were also reports that Cecil Sr. had tried to get schools to pay him for his son to play there. He was accused of contacting Mississippi State specifically.

Auburn officials said they did not pay the Newtons any money and had done nothing wrong. However, in early December of 2010, the school barred Cam from playing. The NCAA had presented evidence that Cecil Newton had asked Mississippi State for more than $100,000 for his son to go there.

One day later, the NCAA determined that Cam could play after all. The NCAA found there was no proof that Cam or Auburn knew what Cecil Sr. was doing.

On the football field, Cam needed to improve his passing skills. He had talent and was eager to learn, so improvement came fast. So did victories. The Tigers kept winning and were the undefeated number one team in the country when they played powerhouse Alabama in November of 2010. The Crimson Tide jumped to a 24-0 lead before Cam rallied Auburn to a 28-27 win. The Tigers won the Southeastern Conference (SEC) title and then the

Cam's late-November performance against powerhouse Alabama might have clinched the 2010 Heisman Trophy for him. He led Auburn back from a 24-0 deficit.

national championship over Oregon, 22-19, as Cam threw for two touchdowns.

Cam was among the nation's top passers and runners, and was the easy winner of the Heisman Trophy, awarded every year to the nation's best college football player. He beat runner-up Andrew Luck of Stanford by nearly 1,100 votes. He also won the Davey O'Brien National Quarterback Award, was named Associated Press All-America (first team), and was the SEC Player of the Year.

Cam had one more year to play college football, but he decided he had done enough.

It was time for the NFL.

Cam and NFL commissioner Roger Goodell were all smiles after Cam was chosen as the number one overall pick in the 2011 NFL draft.

Chapter 3

An NFL Star Is Born

The Carolina Panthers had the NFL's number one draft pick in 2011, thanks to a 2-14 record. (The team with the worst record gets the first draft pick the following year.) There was no doubt they would take Cam. New coach Ron Rivera was looking to rebuild, and he needed a quarterback to lead the way. Cam was the obvious choice.

Before training camp started in July, Cam worked out hard to get ready, and it paid off. He was named the starting quarterback ahead of veterans Derek Anderson and Jimmy Clausen. He also signed a four-year, $22 million contract.

Cam made instant impact. In the season opener, he set a rookie first-game record by throwing for 422 yards and two touchdowns in a road loss to Arizona. The next week he threw for 432 yards in another loss. No rookie had ever thrown for so many yards in the first two games. The 854 passing yards broke the NFL record for most yards thrown in the first two games of a season.

Cam finished the season completing 60.0 percent of his passes for 4,051 yards, 21 touchdowns, and 17 interceptions. He also rushed for 706 yards and 14 touchdowns. Carolina went 6-10. That was four more victories than the previous season, but everyone wanted more.

It took Cam three years to improve enough to make his first NFL Pro Bowl. He likely will be an all-star for years to come.

In Cam's second season, he completed 57.7 percent of his passes for 3,816 yards and 19 touchdowns. He also rushed for 741 yards and eight scores. However, he had 12 interceptions and 10 fumbles. The Panthers finished 7-9.

Cam had a breakthrough in his third season. He led Carolina to a 12-4 record, the NFC South title, and its first playoff appearance in five years. That earned him a spot in the 2014 Pro Bowl, the NFL's version of an all-star game.

In 2014, a series of injuries—ankle surgery, broken ribs, a sore hand, and fractured vertebrae from a car crash—caused Cam to miss two games. Despite the lost time, Cam had a record-breaking fourth season. He led the Panthers to a second straight NFC South title and their first playoff win since 2005. Cam became the first quarterback in NFL history to have at least 3,000 passing yards and 500 rushing yards in four straight seasons, and the first to have at least 10,000 passing yards and at least 2,000 rushing yards after his first four seasons. That was enough for Carolina officials to sign him to a 5-year, $103.8 million contract in July of 2015.

That put even more pressure on Cam, but boy, did he handle it.

Cam was basically unstoppable during the 2015 season. He threw for 3,837 yards with 35 touchdowns and 10 interceptions. He also rushed for 636 yards and 10 touchdowns. No player in NFL history had ever thrown for more than 30 touchdowns and rushed for at least 10 in a season. His 43 career rushing touchdowns were the most ever by an NFL quarterback.

Cam got 48 first-place votes to easily win NFL MVP honors. He also beat out Pittsburgh Steelers receiver Antonio Brown for offensive player of the year. He led Carolina to a 15-1 record, the best in franchise history. The Panthers started 14-0 before losing to Atlanta, 20-13. (Two weeks before, the Panthers had crushed Atlanta, 38-0.)

Cam was at his best in the playoffs, leading the Panthers to wins over Seattle and Arizona. He threw for two touchdowns and rushed for two more in the 49-15 NFC Championship Game win over Arizona. That gave him 50 total touchdowns for the season, and set the stage for what he expected to be a Super Bowl to remember.

As it turned out, he was right—for all the wrong reasons.

Cam was nearly unstoppable in the 2016 NFC title game against Arizona. He threw for two touchdowns and ran for two more. Carolina's 49 points were an NFC championship game record.

Cam and the Panthers finally met their match against Denver's NFL-best defense in the 2016 Super Bowl. The Broncos beat them up physically and mentally, and won the game.

Chapter 4

Super Bowl Lesson

For 18 games Cam played as well as any quarterback had ever played, showing a combination of passing and running the NFL had never seen before. The Panthers came in with a 17-1 record and a powerhouse offense no one had stopped.

Now it came down to one last contest—the Super Bowl, one of the world's biggest sporting events. In this showdown, Carolina and Cam Newton would face the Denver Broncos and aging superstar quarterback Peyton Manning.

Although no one knew it at the time, Manning was set to play the last game of his career. Injuries and age had taken away much of his ability (he lost his starting job for a while), but he was smart and tough enough to lead the Broncos to playoff victories over Pittsburgh and New England.

He and Denver also had one big advantage: the NFL's best defense.

Suddenly, Cam was a target like never before. Carolina's offensive line could not protect him, and he struggled. He threw one interception and fumbled twice. The Broncos returned one fumble for a touchdown. The other fumble set up another Denver touchdown.

The worst moment came in the fourth quarter. Carolina was down only six points when Denver linebacker Von Miller knocked the ball out of Cam's hands. Cam didn't even try to recover the fumble, although he was in position to do so. The Broncos recovered it and went on to score another touchdown.

Cam took a lot of heat for giving up the ball. His excuse? His leg was in a bad position and he didn't want to risk an injury.

"We didn't lose the game because of that fumble," he said.[1]

Overall, Cam was 18-for-41 for 265 yards. Manning wasn't much better (13-for-23, 141 yards, two turnovers), but he didn't need to be. The outstanding Broncos defense made the difference.

Carolina had the NFL's number one offense, but could only score 10 points against Denver. The Panthers had scored at least 30 points 10 times before the Super Bowl, including their previous three games.

After the Super Bowl, Denver quarterback Peyton Manning, a future Hall of Famer, encouraged Cam to keep working. Peyton knew what it was like to lose a Super Bowl. He lost 2 of the 4 Super Bowls he played.

After the game, the quarterbacks talked. Manning told Cam he would have a "great career" and that "I'll be pulling for you. Keep it going."[2]

Cam basically thanked him and said "Yes sir" a lot.[3]

Cam's disastrous post-game press conference followed. Months later, he told *Ebony* that he should have handled it better, and that he let fans and family down.

"I represent something way bigger than myself," he told *Ebony*.

"I just wasn't ready to talk. Was I mad? Heck, yeah! But there could have been a better way to control it, and that's why I think having more time (before the interview) would have helped."[4]

Cam always finds time to meet with fans, especially children. In 2015, he cheered with students as part of the Cam Newton Foundation–sponsored School Spirit Day.

Chapter 5

Beyond the Field

On a warm April morning in 2016, Cam Newton saw a group of North Carolina seventh graders playing football during recess. One of the students was wearing a Cam Newton jersey. Cam couldn't resist. He jumped the fence to play football with them.

His surprise visit left a big impact. A seventh-grade teacher told a local TV station that one young girl was crying with excitement. "She said, 'That was just the best moment of my life.'"[1]

That's the effect Cam has on people. It's one reason he started his Cam Newton Foundation, which is "committed to enhancing the lives of young people by addressing their socioeconomic educational, physical and emotional needs." It specifically helps communities in Atlanta, Georgia, and Charlotte, North Carolina.[2]

The foundation's theme is "Every 1 Matters." That includes three main areas: Every 1 Learns (providing academic support and scholarships), Every 1 Plays (providing chances for play, fitness, and overall good health), and Every 1 Gives (encouraging community service and more).[3]

Cam often works with the Make-A-Wish Foundation. For example, in April 2016, he met 11-year-old Noah. The boy was born with Klippel-Trenaunay syndrome, which caused his left leg to grow abnormally. Cam surprised Noah at school, took him to the Panthers' training facility, then took him bowling and to a Charlotte Hornets basketball game.

In the fall of 2015, Cam surprised another Charlotte-area boy at the boy's Halloween party. A month later, he hosted a Thanksgiving dinner for more than 800 underprivileged kids. He often invites children who are living with cancer to visit him on the sidelines before NFL games.

Cam is known for his great fashion sense. He's been on the cover of *GQ* magazine and has his own clothing line (MADE by Cam Newton). He attends high-profile fashion shows and also does motivational speaking.

He is a man of faith and says that he always takes time to "thank God every day. I'm just his instrument."[4]

Cam is also a father. On December 30, 2015, during Carolina's playoff run, he tweeted that he and longtime girlfriend Kia Proctor had a son, Chosen Sebastian Newton. The baby had been born on December 24, but Cam

Sometimes wishes do come true thanks to the Make-A-Wish Foundation, which got Cam together with 11-year-old Noah, who suffers from a serious disability. Noah's dream was to meet and spend time with Cam. That included a Charlotte Hornets NBA game.

kept it quiet, he said, "because I didn't want to create a distraction for my team."⁵

Finally, Cam kept a promise to his mother. He returned to Auburn and finished his degree in sociology.

"My education was always my mother's top priority," he told *People Magazine* in 2015. "I've always been blessed to have a family that supports me. It's a Biblical quote: 'Iron sharpens iron.' My mother has always been there to sharpen me."⁶

Added Jackie: "He is still part of the Auburn family. He just needs to complete things."⁷

And so Cam has, and so he will. Even Superman never runs out of things to do, worlds to conquer, and championships to win.

Cam understands his responsibility to be a role model for his many young fans. It's a big reason why he started the Cam Newton Foundation.

STATISTICS

Passing

Year	Team	G	Att	Comp	Pct	Att/G	Yds	Avg	Yds/G	TD	TD%	Int	Int%	Lng	20+	40+	Rate
2015	Carolina Panthers	16	495	296	59.8	30.9	3,837	7.8	239.8	35	7.1	10	2.0	74T	52	10	99.4
2014	Carolina Panthers	14	448	262	58.5	32.0	3,127	7.0	223.4	18	4.0	12	2.7	51	37	4	82.1
2013	Carolina Panthers	16	473	292	61.7	29.6	3,379	7.1	211.2	24	5.1	13	2.7	79T	33	7	88.8
2012	Carolina Panthers	16	485	280	57.7	30.3	3,869	8.0	241.8	19	3.9	12	2.5	82	57	11	86.2
2011	Carolina Panthers	16	517	310	60.0	32.3	4,051	7.8	253.2	21	4.1	17	3.3	91T	65	9	84.5
	TOTAL	78	2,418	1,440	59.6	31.0	18,263	7.6	234.1	117	4.8	64	2.6	91	244	41	88.3

Rushing

Year	Team	G	Att	Att/G	Yds	Avg	Yds/G	TD	Lng	1st	1st%	20	40	FUM
2015	Carolina Panthers	16	132	8.2	636	4.8	39.8	10	47	56	42.4	3	1	4
2014	Carolina Panthers	14	103	7.4	539	5.2	38.5	5	22	45	43.7	2	0	3
2013	Carolina Panthers	16	111	6.9	585	5.3	36.6	6	56	45	40.5	2	1	1
2012	Carolina Panthers	16	127	7.9	741	5.8	46.3	8	72T	49	38.6	9	2	4
2011	Carolina Panthers	16	126	7.9	706	5.6	44.1	14	49T	51	40.5	6	1	2
	TOTAL	78	599	7.7	3207	5.4	41.1	43	72	246	41.1	22	5	14

CHRONOLOGY

1989 Cameron Jerrell Newton is born on May 11 in College Park, a city near Atlanta, Georgia.

2003 Cam becomes a starter at Atlanta's Westlake High School.

2007 He enrolls at the University of Florida; plays for the Gators for two seasons.

2009 In January, Newton leaves Florida and enrolls at Blinn College in Texas. That fall he leads Blinn to the junior college national championship. He takes official recruiting visits to Mississippi State and to Auburn University in Alabama. Auburn offers him a scholarship.

2010 In April, Newton is named starting quarterback for Auburn. In July, the SEC notifies Auburn that Cam's father, Cecil Newton, is suspected of improper recruitment for soliciting money from Mississippi State. Auburn begins an investigation; the NCAA ultimately rules that Cam is eligible to play. On September 4, Newton accounts for five touchdowns and 357 yards in a 52-26 season-opening win over Arkansas State. He is named offensive player of the week six times; he wins the Heisman Trophy as the nation's best player.

2011 On January 10, he leads Auburn to a 22-19 win over Oregon for the national championship. In April the Carolina Panthers make him the NFL's number one pick. He signs a four-year, $22 million contract. On opening day, Newton breaks Peyton Manning's NFL rookie record for most passing yards by throwing for 422 yards in a 28-21 loss to Arizona.

2012 Newton is named to his first Pro Bowl and wins AP offensive rookie of the year. He sets the NFL rookie record by throwing for 4,051 yards.

2013 Newton leads Carolina to a 12-4 record and the NFL playoffs. He is again selected to the Pro Bowl.

2015 He wins the NFL most valuable player award. His contract is renewed for five years at $103.8 million. He leads Carolina to a 14-1 start and then the Super Bowl. He becomes a dad when son Chosen Sebastian Newton is born on December 24.

2016 Cam leads Carolina to a 14-0 start and a 15-1 regular season record. The Panthers finish 17-2 after losing to Denver in the Super Bowl. Cam wins the NFL's MVP award after having one of the best seasons ever by a quarterback. He totals 45 touchdowns, including 35 by pass, and only 10 interceptions.

CHAPTER NOTES

Chapter 1
1. Cam Newton Super Bowl Transcript. February 7, 2016.
2. Busbee, Jay. "Deion Sanders Lights Up Cam Newton: 'You Can't Do That.'" *Yahoo Sports*, February 8, 2016.
3. Chadiha, Jeffri. "Cam Newton's Antics in Super Bowl 50 Loss Fuel Criticism." NFL.com, February 8, 2016.
4. Dator, James. "Cam Newton Explains Why He Didn't Jump on His Fumble Late in the Super Bowl." *SB Nation*, February 9, 2016.
5. Inabinett, Mark. "Broncos Cornerback Says He Didn't Know Cam Newton Could Hear Him after Super Bowl." AL.com Sports, April 23, 2016.
6. Newton, David. "Cam Newton Defends Walking Out of News Conference." *ESPN*, February 11, 2016.
7. Newton, David. "Celebrating Cam Newton's 27th Birthday with 27 Memorable Quotes." ESPN, May 11, 2016.

Chapter 2
1. Newton, Cam. "My Path to the Pros." ESPN, June 26, 2013.
2. Ibid.

Chapter 4
1. Dator, James. "Cam Newton Explains Why He Didn't Jump on His Fumble Late in the Super Bowl." *SB Nation*, February 9, 2016.
2. Brinson, Will. "Here Was Peyton Manning's Message to Cam Newton after Super Bowl 50." CBS Sports.com, February 15, 2016.
3. Ibid.
4. Newton, David. "Cam Newton Says He Let People Down with Post-Super Bowl News Conference." ESPN, April 28, 2016.

Chapter 5
1. Breech, John. "Look: Cam Newton Shocks School Kids by Hopping Fence to Play Football." CBS Sports.com, April 23, 2016.
2. Cam Newton Foundation.
3. Ibid.
4. Newton, Cam. "My Path to the Pros." ESPN, June 26, 2013.
5. Jones, Jonathan. "Panthers QB Cam Newton Announces Birth of Son." *Charlotte Observer*, December 30, 2015.
6. Amato, Laura. "Cam Newton's Family: The Pictures You Need to See." Heavy.com, January 24, 2016.
7. Ibid.

FURTHER READING

Books

Charlotte Observer, The. *Super Cam: Cam Newton's Rise to Panthers Greatness.* Chicago: Triumph Books, Chicago, 2016.

Coach Jeff. *Cam Newton Quiz Book—50 Fun & Fact Filled Questions about One of Greatest QB in The NFL: Cam Newton.* Kindle Edition.

Dawkins, Richard. *Cam Newton Biography.* Kindle Edition. 2015.

Fishman, John. *Cam Newton.* Minneapolis: Learner Publishing Group, 2016.

Johnson, Joe. *Cam Newton: The NFL Star's Life and Career.* Kindle Edition. 2012.

Waters, Alison. *Cam Newton.* CreateSpace Publishing, 2016.

On the Internet

Cam Newton Foundation: https://www.cam1newton.com

Works Consulted

Amato, Laura. "Cam Newton's Family: The Pictures You Need to See." *Heavy.com,* February 5, 2016. http://heavy.com/sports/2016/01/cam-newton-family-girlfriend-wife-kia-proctor-son-chosen-mom-dad-instagram-pictures-twitter-panthers-nfl/2/

Bishop, Greg. "Von Trapped." *Sports Illustrated,* February 15, 2016.

Breech, John. "Look: Cam Newton Shocks School Kids by Hopping Fence to Play Football." CBS Sports.com, April 23, 2016. http://www.cbssports.com/nfl/eye-on-football/25564711/look-cam-newton-shocks-school-kids-by-hopping-fence-to-play-football

Brinson, Will. "Here Was Peyton Manning's Message to Cam Newton after Super Bowl 50." CBS Sports.com, February 15, 2016. http://www.cbssports.com/nfl/eye-on-football/25484423/here-was-peyton-mannings-message-to-cam-newton-following-super-bowl-50

Brinson, Will. "Why Are Cam Newton, Panthers Doing the Dab? A History of the Dance Craze." CBS Sports.com, January 31, 2016. http://www.cbssports.com/nfl/eye-on-football/25467958/why-are-cam-newton-panthers-doing-the-dab-a-history-of-the-dance-craze

Busbee, Jay. "Deion Sanders Lights Up Cam Newton: 'You Can't Do That.'" *Yahoo Sports,* NFL Network postgame commentary. http://sports.yahoo.com/blogs/nfl-shutdown-corner/deion-sanders-lights-up-cam-newton---you-can-t-do-that-055241681.html

Cam Newton Stats and Bio, Carolina Panthers. http://www.panthers.com/team/roster/cam-newton/a9ff8c76-7a6a-4e1a-9e9a-b72aff45deb4/

Cam Newton Super Bowl Transcript. ESPN, February 7, 2016. http://espn.go.com/nfl/story/_/id/14737633/transcript-cam-newton-postgame-comments-nfl

Chadiha, Jeffri. "Cam Newton's Antics in Super Bowl 50 Loss Fuel Criticism." NFL.com, February 8, 2016. http://www.nfl.com/news/story/0ap3000000634557/article/cam-newtons-antics-in-super-bowl-50-loss-fuel-criticism

PHOTO CREDITS: P. 1—Parker Anderson; p. 6—Michael DeJesus; p. 7—Thibous, Robert Donovan; p. 13—Matthew Tosh; p. 16—A. Martinez; p. 16—Dwayne; pp. 18, 20—Arnie Papp; pp. 22, 25—Grant Baldwin. All other photos—Public Domain. Every measure has been taken to find all copyright holders of material used in this book. In the event any mistakes or omissions have happened within, attempts to correct them will be made in future editions of the book.

FURTHER READING

Dator, James. "Cam Newton Explains Why He Didn't Jump on His Fumble Late in the Super Bowl." *SB Nation*, February 9, 2016. http://www.sbnation.com/lookit/2016/2/9/10951142/cam-newton-explains-fumble-didnt-dive-von-miller-super-bowl-broncos-panthers

Durkee, Travis. "Cam Newton Makes Another Kid's Wish Come True." *Omnisport*, April 30, 2016. http://www.sportingnews.com/nfl-news/4703916-cam-newton-kids-charity-make-a-wish-noah-carolina-panthers-dab

Glier, Ray, and Pete Thamel. "Newton Faced Suspension at Florida." *New York Times*, November 9, 2010. http://www.nytimes.com/2010/11/10/sports/ncaafootball/10auburn.html

Inabinett, Mark. "Broncos Cornerback Says He Didn't Know Cam Newton Could Hear Him after Super Bowl." *AL.com Sports*, April 23, 2016. http://www.al.com/sports/index.ssf/2016/04/broncos_cornerback_says_he_did.html

Jones, Jonathan. "Panthers QB Cam Newton Announces Birth of Son." Charlotte Observer, December 30, 2015. http://www.charlotteobserver.com/sports/nfl/carolina-panthers/article52361270.html

Klemko, Robert. "How Super Bowl QBs View Cam's Choice Not to Dive." *Sports Illustrated MMQB*, February 11, 2016. http://mmqb.si.com/mmqb/2016/02/10/cam-newton-dive-fumble-super-bowl-50-carolina-panthers-nfl

Newton, Cam. "My Path to the Pros." ESPN, June 26, 2013. http://espn.go.com/nfl/story/_/id/9407038/carolina-panthers-cam-newton-path-pros-espn-magazine

Newton, David. "Cam Newton Defends Walking Out of News Conference." *ESPN*, February 11, 2016. http://espn.go.com/nfl/story/_/id/14745754/super-bowl-50-cam-newton-carolina-panthers-defends-walking-reporters

Newton, David. "Cam Newton Says He Let People Down with Post-Super Bowl News Conference." ESPN, April 28, 2016. http://espn.go.com/blog/carolina-panthers/post/_/id/20561/cam-newton-tells-ebony-he-let-down-his-fans-and-family-with-post-super-bowl-press-conference

Newton, David. "Celebrating Cam Newton's 27th Birthday with 27 Memorable Quotes." ESPN, May 11, 2016. http://espn.go.com/blog/carolina-panthers/post/_/id/20724/celebrating-cam-newtons-27th-birthday-with-27-memorable-quotes

Wilco, Daniel. "Chasing Superman: Caylin Newton's Life as Cam's Brother and His Journey to Become Something More." *SEC Country*, January 2016. https://www.seccountry.com/sec-news/chasing-superman-caylin-newtons-life-as-cams-brother-and-his-journey-to-become-something-more

GLOSSARY

arrogance (AYR-oh-gunts)—The feeling of being better than others.

burglary (BUR-gluh-ree)—Breaking into a home to take someone else's property.

championship (CHAM-pee-un-ship)—A game that determines the best team in a given sport.

deficit (DEH-fih-sit)—Disadvantage, short of points.

errant (AIR-ant)—Off course.

franchise (FRAN-chyz)—A sports team and its organization.

fumble (FUM-bul)—In football, to drop the ball.

Heisman Trophy (HYS-man TROH-fee)—An award given to the best player in college football each year.

interception (in-ter-SEP-shun)—In football, a pass caught by a defensive player from the other team.

Klippel-Trenaunay syndrome (KLIP-ul tray-NOH-nay SIN-drohm)—A condition that is present at birth that affects a person's blood vessels, bones, and soft tissues.

larceny (LAR-seh-nee)—Taking someone else's personal property.

MVP—Most Valuable Player.

NCAA—National Collegiate (kuh-LEE-jit) Athletic Association: The organization that regulates college sports.

NFL—National Football League: The organization that oversees professional football in the United States.

NFL Draft—A multiday period in April when NFL teams select the best college players for their teams.

obstruction of justice (ub-STRUK-shun of JUS-tis)—An act that keeps police from doing their jobs.

Pro Bowl—The NFL All-Star game that honors the league's best players.

prospect (PRAH-spekt)—A young player who has the ability to be successful at a higher level.

quarterback (KWOR-ter-bak)—In football, the player who leads the offense, either by passing, running, or handing the ball to his teammates.

scholarship (SKAH-lur-ship)—An award of money to attend school based on athletic or academic achievements.

SEC—The Southeastern Conference: A group of teams from southern colleges that compete against one another in a variety of sports.

socioeconomic (soh-she-oh-ek-kuh-NAH-mik)—A combination of social and money factors.

varsity (VAR-sih-tee)—The team with the more seasoned players.

vertebra (VER-teh-bruh)—One of the bones in the spine.

INDEX

Allen, Dallas 10
Auburn University 11, 12, 13, 25
Blinn College 12, 27
Brown, Antonio 17
Cam Newton Foundation 23, 25
Camp Creek Middle School 9
Carolina Panthers 5, 15, 16, 17, 19, 24
Chizik, Gene 12
Culpepper, Dante 12
Davey O'Brien National Quarterback Award 13
Denver Broncos 5, 19, 20
Florida Gators 11, 12, 27
Goodell, Roger 15
Harris, Chris 5
Heisman Trophy 7, 13
Klippel-Trenaunay syndrome 23
Luck, Andrew 13
Make-A-Wish Foundation 23
Manning, Peyton 19, 20, 21
Meyer, Urban 12
Miller, Von 19
Mississippi State 12, 27
NCAA 12
Newton, Cam
    awards 5, 7, 13, 16, 17
    birth 9
    charity 23–25
    injuries 11, 16
    education 9, 10, 11, 12
    records 15, 16, 17, 26
Newton, Caylin (brother) 9
Newton, Cecil, Jr. (brother) 8, 9, 10
Newton, Cecil, Sr. (father) 8, 9, 12
Newton, Chosen Sebastian (son) 24, 27
Newton, Jackie (mother) 9, 25
NFC Championship Game 17
Pro Bowl 16
Proctor, Kia 24
Rivera, Ron 7, 15
Rose, Jalen 6
Sanders, Deion 6
Seaborn Lee Elementary School 9, 10
Southeastern Conference 13
Super Bowl 5–7, 17, 18, 19–21
Tebow, Tim 11
Tuberville, Tommy 11
Westlake High School 10
Young, Vince 12

26 50

RECEIVED JUN 1 9 2017